# Record-Setting
# Animals

Written and illustrated by

## Melinda Bergman Burgener

Sierra Club Books / Little, Brown and Company
San Francisco      Boston · Toronto

*For my dear mother, Sylvia Davis, who is still setting records.*

*Special thanks to Jim Glenn (who knows his way around Grzimek's like nobody's business) for his impeccable research and collaboration.*

The Sierra Club, founded in 1892 by John Muir, has devoted itself to the study and protection of the earth's scenic and ecological resources — mountains, wetlands, woodlands, wild shores and rivers, deserts and plains. The publishing program of the Sierra Club offers books to the public as a nonprofit educational service in the hope that they may enlarge the public's understanding of the Club's basic concerns. The Sierra Club has some sixty chapters in the United States and in Canada. For information about how you may participate in its programs to preserve wilderness and the quality of life, please address inquiries to Sierra Club, 730 Polk Street, San Francisco, CA 94109.

A Pale Bluestocking Production

First Edition

Some of the illustrations that appear in this book are adapted from previously published photographs or drawings.

Albatross: courtesy K. Kenyon/Photo Researchers. Ant: courtesy Ross E. Hutchins/ Photo Researchers. Anteater and sloth: from *Armadillos, Anteaters and Sloths* by Jane E. Hartman, courtesy Holiday House, Inc. Bat: courtesy M. P. L. Fogden/ Bruce Coleman, Inc. Cheetah: courtesy Frans Lanting, photographer. Condor: courtesy George Laycock, from *The World's Endangered Wildlife.* Eagle: from *Eagles* by Joe Van Wormer, © 1985, courtesy E. P. Dutton. Flea: used by permission from *A Golden Guide/Insects,* illustrated by J.G. Irving, © 1956 Western Publishing Co., Inc. Frog: courtesy A. Blank/Bruce Coleman, Inc. Python: courtesy Pittsburgh Zoo, William B. Allen, Jr., photographer. Silkworm moth larva: used by permission from *A Golden Guide/Butterflies and Moths,* illustrated by A. Durenceau, © 1977 Western Publishing Co., Inc. Walkingstick: from *Field Book of Insects* by F. E. Lutz, courtesy G. P. Putnam's Sons.

Library of Congress Catalog Card Number: 88-80667

10 9 8 7 6 5 4 3 2 1

Sierra Club Books/Little, Brown children's books are published by Little, Brown and Company (Inc.) in association with Sierra Club Books

Published simultaneously in Canada
by Little, Brown & Company (Canada) Limited

Printed in Hong Kong by South China Printing

# Introducing the Animals

Some of us know which is the largest land mammal. But who can name the smallest? Or the silliest-looking? Or the best bird baby-sitter? Or the most poisonous fish? Or the deadliest animal on earth?

Sierra Club WILDCARDS introduce you to these title-holders and to many other Olympians of the animal world. Each of these record-setters is truly "one in a million," because there are more than a million different kinds of animals known in the world today. Although every one is special, the forty-eight featured in this book are real stars, each in its own way.

Our animal celebrities certainly didn't enter any contests. For one thing, it would difficult to make such a competition fair. Big hulking beetles shouldn't have to sign up on the same list as elephants to be judged for most impressive size. Both are

remarkable, but on very different scales! It makes more sense to sort animals into different groups, and in fact, that's just what scientists do. To begin with, they divide animals into two major groups, *vertebrates* and *invertebrates*. Vertebrates are animals with backbones: fish, birds, reptiles, amphibians, and mammals. All animals without backbones are invertebrates; insects, spiders, and jellyfish are familiar examples.

Categories such as "fish" or "mammals" are called *classes*. We humans are a *species* within the class of mammals (*species* is another word for "kind" or "sort" or "type"). Because mammals are often impressively large and very noticeable — like whales, gorillas, and giraffes, for example — you might think there are more species of mammals than there are of other animal classes. If so, the chart below will surprise you!

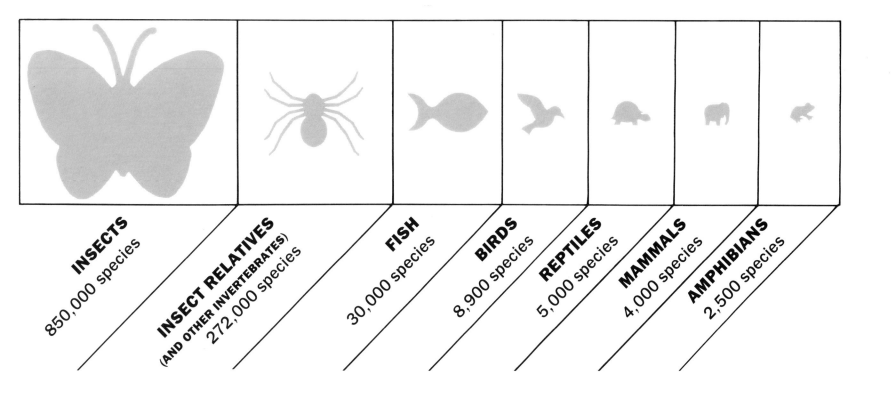

INSECTS
850,000 species

INSECT RELATIVES
(AND OTHER INVERTEBRATES)
272,000 species

FISH
30,000 species

BIRDS
8,900 species

REPTILES
5,000 species

MAMMALS
4,000 species

AMPHIBIANS
2,500 species

You will find the game cards in this book divided into animal classes or, in two cases, combinations of classes. The list below describes some of the characteristics of the members of those classes:

**MAMMALS** breathe air and are warm-blooded. Most species have fur (or hair), and most give birth to live young (the two exceptions lay eggs). All female mammals produce milk for their young. Monkeys, rats, bats, whales, and your neighbors are mammals.

**BIRDS**, too, are warm-blooded. They are the only animals with feathers. All birds lay eggs. Most can fly. Some, however, have lost this ability over the centuries, and either remain on the ground like the ostrich or swim about in the water like the penguin. Ducks, parakeets, pigeons, and boobies are birds.

**REPTILES** are cold-blooded animals, usually covered with armor of scales or bony plates. Most species live on land, but many spend much or even all of their time in the water. They either crawl on their bellies or move on short legs. Alligators, lizards, snakes, and turtles are reptiles. Dinosaurs were.

**AMPHIBIANS** have characteristics of both reptiles and fish. When they are young, most amphibians live in water and breathe with gills. As they mature, they develop lungs and become air breathers. Amphibians don't have scales. Frogs, toads, and salamanders are group members.

**FISH** spend their entire existence in water (look for the record-setting exception). These cold-blooded animals breathe with gills, steer themselves by means of fins, and are usually covered with scales. Most species live either in salt water or in fresh water; a few are happy in both. Sharks, eels, tuna, and seahorses are fish.

**INSECTS** outnumber all the other kinds of animals put together — and more species are discovered each year! They were among the first land animals, appearing about four hundred million years ago. Insects, like all invertebrates, are cold-blooded. They often have six legs, and their bodies are usually divided into three segments. We see many insects every day; flies, fleas, ants, bees, and butterflies are examples.

**INSECT RELATIVES,** for our purposes, are invertebrates that are not true insects. These creatures actually belong to many different animal classes, each with its own special name. Spiders, scorpions, crabs, and millipedes all fit into our insect relative group.

You can be sure that just listing and sorting out all the animal types is a huge job. Some biologists work full-time at it, and there are still many questions with fuzzy answers.

There is no question at all, though, about the superlative traits and uncanny abilities of the forty-eight record-setting animals featured on the following pages. So look over the cards, remove them to form a deck, and choose a game from the next section. Then get ready to play cards and be amazed!

# Games

In 1643, when a five-year-old boy was crowned King Louis XIV of France, his mother had a series of game cards designed to teach him his studies. Other royal tutors followed suit and wrote facts on pretty hand-painted cards, so the young princes and princesses could learn their lessons through play. There were cards to teach many different subjects — foreign languages and astronomy, mathematics and music.

Throughout history, people have played cards to learn new things, sharpen their minds, and just have fun!

Described below are fourteen games to play with your set of forty-eight WILDCARDS. The games are divided into three skill levels — beginner, intermediate, and advanced. The best way to find out which level suits you is to try one game from each level. You might enjoy them all!

Before playing the games, you may want to read all the cards and become familiar with the animals. You'll also need to keep the following in mind:

- "Kinds" or "categories" refer to animals with the same border color. Here are the five border colors and the class (or classes) of animals included in each:

  Yellow — mammals
  Blue — birds
  Orange — reptiles and amphibians
  Green — fish
  Purple — insects and insect relatives

- A "pair" is two cards with the same border color; "3 of a kind" is three cards with the same color.

- Unless otherwise noted, play always moves in a clockwise direction.

In addition to the amazing record set by the animal, each card contains many other facts to inform and entertain you. So play your cards right and learn all about record-setting animals!

## *Solo Games*

## 1. Animal Solitaire

**Skill level:** Beginner.

**Object:** To end up with 5 columns of cards, each column a different color.

Shuffle the deck and deal out 5 cards face up, side by side. Put all cards of the same border color in one column. Draw a new card from the top of the deck. Depending on the color of the card, either begin a new column or add to an existing one. Continue until the deck is played out. (In Animal Solitaire you're always a winner!)

## 2. Three's a Crowd

**Skill level:** Intermediate.

**Object:** To remove all the cards from the table — or to come as close as you can.

Shuffle the deck and deal out 4 cards face up in a row. If any 3 cards that are next to each other are of the same category (have the same border color), remove them, put them to the side, and deal 3 new cards in their place. If no 3 adjacent cards are of the same category, add a fifth card on the right end of the row. If that doesn't help, add a sixth card, and so on, until 3 in a row can be removed. (Your chances of removing all the cards are excellent!)

## 3. Mathemanimals

**Skill level:** Advanced.

**Object:** To remove all the cards from the table — or to come as close as you can.

Shuffle the deck and deal out 4 cards face up in a row. If the numbers on any 3 cards that are next to each other add up to 10, 20, or 30, remove those cards, put them to the side, and deal 3 new cards in their place. If no 3 adjacent cards add up to 10, 20, or 30, add a fifth card on the right end of the row. If that doesn't help, add a sixth card, and so on, until 3 in a row can be removed. (This is a difficult game to win.)

# Games for More than One Player

## 4. Old Tortoise

**Skill level:** Beginner.

**Players:** 2 or more.

**Object:** Not to get stuck holding the Old Tortoise at the end of the game.

Before starting, remove from the deck all reptiles and amphibians except for the Tortoise. Shuffle and deal out all the other cards (some players may have an extra card). Each player then sorts his or her cards for pairs and discards these pairs face up in a pile in the center. The dealer starts by picking one card from the hand of the player to his or her left. (Keep the backs of your cards well covered while the player next to you is picking from your hand.) If that card matches one in the dealer's hand, the dealer discards that pair face up in the pile and takes another turn. If the card doesn't make a pair, it is added to the dealer's hand, and the next player takes a turn. The game is over when all the cards are paired and one player is left holding the Old Tortoise.

## 5. Go Fish

**Skill level:** Beginner.

**Players:** 2 to 5.

**Object:** To collect the most sets of 3 of a kind.

Shuffle the deck and deal out 4 cards to each player. Spread out the rest of the cards, face down; this is the "fish pond." The dealer begins by asking any other player for a card in a particular category — for example, "Do you have any reptiles or amphibians?" (Be sure to keep your card backs well covered.) If the player has a card with an orange border, he or she must give it to the dealer. But when a player is asked and doesn't have the requested card, he or she says "Go fish." The dealer must then close his eyes and pick a card from the fish pond. If it is a card of the requested category, the dealer shows it to the other players and gets to fish for another card. If it is not, the dealer's turn is over, and the next player tries. During his or her turn, each player discards any sets of 3 of a kind and places them face up in a pile in front of him or her. Each player takes a turn until all

the cards are collected into sets of 3. If a player runs out of cards before the fish pond is empty, she or he may continue to play by selecting 4 new cards from the pond. The game ends when all the players are out of cards and the fish pond has "dried up." The winner is the player who has the most sets of 3 of a kind.

## 6. Animal Concentration

**Skill level:** Beginner.

**Players:** 2 or more.

**Object:** To collect the most pairs.

Shuffle all 48 cards and spread them out face down, leaving a little space between them. The first player turns over any 2 cards and calls out the animal, category, and color of each. If the two cards match (by color), the player takes the pair and turns over 2 more cards, and so on. If they don't match, they are turned back over in place, and the next player tries for a pair. The winner is the player who takes the greatest number of pairs. (A good memory helps!)

## 7. Flea, Fly, Frog

**Skill level:** Intermediate.

**Players:** 3 or more.

**Object:** To collect all 48 cards.

Shuffle the deck and deal out all 48 cards (some players may have an extra card). Place all your cards face down in a stack in front of you. Keep one hand covering your stack. Use your other hand *only* for both turning over and slapping cards. The dealer starts by putting her or his top card face up in the middle of the table. Each player, in turn, places her or his top card on top of the middle stack in such a way that all the players can see it at the same time. If the flea, the fly, or the frog is turned up, the first player to slap it wins the pile of cards in the middle. These are placed face down at the bottom of the winner's own deck. The winner then starts the play again by putting her or his top card in the middle. If a card is slapped incorrectly, the "slapper" must give her or his next card to the player whose card was slapped. If a player runs out of cards, that player is eliminated from the game, unless she or he is the first to slap the very next flea, fly, or frog. The game ends when one player has collected all 48 cards. (The faster this game goes, the more exciting it gets. But remember that only one card at a time is placed on the stack in the middle!)

**Tongue Twister Bonus:** try saying "flea, fly, frog" very fast, three times in a row!

## 8. Tuatara

**Skill level:** Intermediate.

**Players:** 3 to 5.

**Object:** Not to be the last one to put your finger on your third eye.

Remove from the deck one set of 4 of a kind for each player (each set from a different category). You will play only with these. (If there are 3 players, you'll use only 12 cards; if there are 4 players, you'll use 16 cards; if there are 5 players, you'll use 20.) Shuffle these cards and deal them out evenly. Players begin by sorting their cards into categories. Each player then discards one card and places it face down on the table. At the same time, all players pass these discarded cards to the player on their left. Each player picks up the passed card and, if it matches one in his or her hand, keeps it and chooses a different card to pass. Keep your eyes on the other players and continue to pass cards (always at the same time). When you get 4 of a kind, without saying a word, put your finger on your forehead. When other players see this, they will put their fingers on their foreheads, too. The last one to realize that a player has collected 4 of a kind will be the last to put his finger on his forehead — just like the lonely tuatara, the last of its kind!

## 9. Crittercross

**Skill level:** Intermediate.

**Players:** 2.

**Object:** To collect the most cards.

Shuffle the deck and deal it out evenly. Put your cards face down in a stack in front of you. Cover the stack with your hand. With your other hand, at the same time as your opponent, turn the top card from your stack face up and place it in the middle of the table. The first one to name a "crittercross" wins that match and keeps that set of cards. A crittercross is made by combining the first letters of one animal name with the last letters of the other. (For example, an albatross and elephant crittercross might be an "eletross" or an "albaphant.") Use your imagination to make up the silliest names as quickly as you can. At the end of the game, the one who has collected the most cards wins.

## 10. Spiders and Beetles

**Skill level:** Intermediate.

**Players:** 2 to 4.

**Object:** To be the first player to run out of cards.

Shuffle the deck and deal 5 cards to each player. Place the remaining cards face down in the middle of the table. Turn over the top card and place it next to the rest of the deck. This is the "starter" card. (If it is a beetle or a spider, put it back in the middle of the deck and turn up a new starter.) The first player must cover the starter with a card that is of the same category as the starter. Each player, in turn, does the same. If a player is unable to cover the starter card, she or he draws cards from the deck until one that can be played is drawn. Spiders and beetles (there are two of each in the deck) are wild cards and can be played no matter what card needs to be covered. When a wild card is used, the player using it must call out the category for the next card. If the category called is birds, for example, the next card played must either be a bird or another wild card. The first player to run out of cards wins. If the drawing deck is used up before a player runs out of cards, shuffle the pile of used cards (leave the last card up as the starter) and continue until someone runs out of cards.

## 11. Animal Acts

**Skill level:** Intermediate and Advanced.

**Players:** 3 or more.

**Object:** To get the other players to guess an animal by acting out its record.

Place all the WILDCARDS in a box or a large bowl. One person acts as timekeeper and scorekeeper. Without looking, each player in turn draws a card and has 3 minutes to act out the record set by the animal on the card so that the other players can guess the name of that animal. If someone guesses correctly, the actor keeps the card and gets 3 points; the guesser receives 2 points. If no one can guess it, the card goes back to the bottom of the box for replay later. The turn then moves on to the next player. When the game stops (be sure everyone has had an equal number of turns), the player with the most points wins!

# 12. Animal Essence

**Skill level:** Advanced.

**Players:** 2 or more.

**Object:** To collect the most cards.

Place all the WILDCARDS in a box or a large bowl. The first player picks a card and hides it from view. The other players get 7 questions between them to figure out which card it is. The questions must have yes or no answers. It's best to start out with basic questions ("Is it a bird?") and then narrow them down ("Does it fly?" "Does it smell bad?"). A player who guesses correctly after asking a question gets to keep that card and draw the next one. If no one guesses correctly after 7 questions have been asked, the card is revealed and the back of it is read out loud. The original player keeps the card and gets to draw the next one. At the end of the game, the player holding the most cards wins. (Make sure you've read your WILDCARDS before playing this game!)

# 13. Big, Bigger, Biggest

**Skill level:** Advanced.

**Players:** 2 or more.

**Object:** To collect all 48 cards.

Shuffle the deck and deal out all 48 cards (some players may have an extra card). Players place their cards face down in a stack in front of them. All players, at the same time, turn up their top cards. The player whose animal is the biggest wins the round. (For example, if the cards are the hummingbird, the pygmy shrew, and the goliath beetle, the beetle wins!) The win-ner of each round collects the others' cards and places them at the bottom of his or her own stack. If 2 or more animals are the same size, or if it cannot be determined which animal is biggest based on information on the front and back of the cards, the players whose cards are involved play a "record breaker": they take the next cards from their stacks and turn them face up. The player whose animal is the biggest wins those cards plus the ones underneath. If the "record breaker" ends in a tie, the players continue to turn up cards until a winner finally takes the whole pile. If a card shows a size *range* for an animal, the *maximum* size is used in this game. Players who run out of cards are eliminated from play. The game is over when one player collects all 48 cards.

# 14. Face the Facts

**Skill level:** Advanced.

**Players:** 3 or more.

**Object:** To collect the most cards.

Shuffle the deck and place it face up in the center. The first player draws the top card, holds it face out to the others, and calls, "Face the facts!" Each player in turn has a chance to recite a fact about that animal. The first one to recite a correct fact keeps the card. (Facts not on the cards are acceptable if they can be checked in a close-at-hand reference book, such as a dictionary or encyclopedia.) If no one recalls a fact about the animal, the original player reads all of the facts out loud and returns the card to the bottom of the deck so that it can be played again later. The player who has collected the most cards when the deck is gone wins.

# RECORD-SETTING Mammals 🐘

MAMMALS

**1**

## Porcupine
**WHERE FOUND:** WORLDWIDE EXCEPT AUSTRALIA
**LENGTH:** 1½ TO 2½ FEET
**WEIGHT:** 15 TO 60 POUNDS

**2**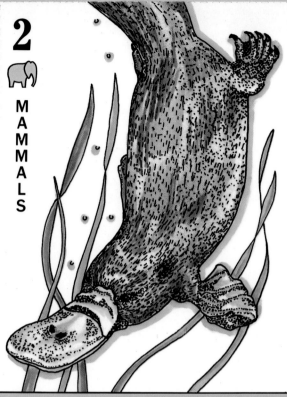

## Platypus
**WHERE FOUND:** AUSTRALIA
**LENGTH:** 2 FEET
**WEIGHT:** 2½ to 4 POUNDS

**3**

## Giant Anteater
**WHERE FOUND:** SOUTH AMERICA
**LENGTH:** 5½ to 7½ FEET
**WEIGHT:** 17 TO 50 POUNDS

**4**

## African Elephant
**WHERE FOUND:** AFRICA
**HEIGHT:** UP TO 13 FEET
**WEIGHT:** UP TO 6 TONS

**5**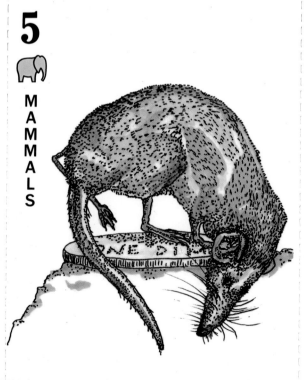

## Savi's Pygmy Shrew
**WHERE FOUND:** MEDITERRANEAN, AFRICA, ASIA
**LENGTH:** 2¼ INCHES
**WEIGHT:** LESS THAN 1/10 OF AN OUNCE

**6**

## Saint Bernard
**WHERE FOUND:** WORLDWIDE
**HEIGHT:** 2½ TO 3½ FEET
**WEIGHT:** 160 TO 295 POUNDS

# Here's the Record:

### Longest Tongue
The tongue of the giant anteater can grow to be 2 feet long!

## Did You Know?

When this 50-pound anteater sticks out its world-record tongue, there's a good reason: it's trying to haul in a mouthful of ants. Once the anteater has torn its way into an anthill using its powerful claws, the creature's sticky tongue picks up the tasty items inside — often along with some of the nest's wreckage. This is a messy way to eat, but the anteater has no teeth at all, so its tongue must do the whole job. Having no fixed home, the anteater follows its keen nose from meal to meal and sleeps in any old hollow log.

## Think of This!

Next time you're at the zoo, notice that an anteater walks oddly — on the knuckles of its forelegs!

# Here's the Record:

### Silliest-Looking Animal
The 2-foot-long platypus is so amazingly unlike any other animal that scientists refused at first to believe it was real!

## Did You Know?

When the first platypus skin reached Europe in the 1800s, zoologists called it a hoax. Not until a complete specimen arrived, years later, was the world prepared to believe in a furry, toothless animal with a leathery duck bill, webbed feet, a beaver tail, poison-tipped spurs, and the innards of an advanced reptile. Oh, and to top it all off, the platypus lays eggs!

## Think of This!

You might be thinking that the platypus owns one of the world's sillier names, too. Actually, *platypous* is Greek for "flat-footed."

# Here's the Record:

### Best Defense
Porcupine quills discourage all enemies.

## Did You Know?

A porcupine "faces" its enemies with its back turned to them. Some porcupine species merely bristle in this menacing position, but the 60-pound giants of Africa actually run backward at their targets. Although no porcupine can shoot its quills, even a light touch will sink the needle-sharp weapons into an overly curious intruder. Quills of the American porcupine are barbed, like tiny harpoons, so they remain stuck and can cause festering wounds.

## Think of This!

Have you heard the expression "Up a creek without a paddle"? That's what you might be if a porcupine is around. They love to gnaw on bare wood, like canoe paddles!

# Here's the Record:

### Heaviest Dog
The noble Saint Bernard may weigh as much as 295 pounds!

## Did You Know?

Ancient Romans brought huge mastiff dogs from Asia to Europe, and it is from this old breed that Saint Bernards descended. Famous as rescuers of lost or snowbound people in the Swiss Alps, Saint Bernards have saved more than 2,500 lives since they began their cold mountain patrols in the 1700s. They have traditionally worked in pairs: one fetches help while the other stays to warm and protect the nearly frozen traveler.

## Think of This!

Around 1800, a terrible disease nearly destroyed the entire breed. Only three Saint Bernards lived — so it's safe to say that any you happen to meet today has ancestors named Pallas and either Barry or Pluto (the three survivors).

# Here's the Record:

### Smallest Land Mammal
Only 2¼ inches long from nose to tail, a Savi's shrew weighs less than a dime!

## Did You Know?

This tiny hunter of mice and insects wouldn't even fill the space you'd need to write out its full name. And its pygmy babies wouldn't stretch past the first three letters!

For its size, the pygmy shrew has the biggest appetite in the animal world. It can devour its own weight in food every 3 hours.

## Think of This!

How much would *you* have to consume in order to eat your weight in food each day? Try about 320 peanut butter and jelly sandwiches!

# Here's the Record:

### Biggest Teeth
An elephant's tusks are actually overgrown teeth. They may grow to be as long as 11 feet, 5 inches!

## Did You Know?

Tusks are not at all the same as horns, which grow from bone in an animal's skull. Tusks are true teeth, firmly rooted in an elephant's upper jaw. Elephants use these 200-pound teeth to root around for food. They also stick them into the ground to support their heavy heads when they nap standing up!

## Think of This!

You may know some other land-animal records that the elephant holds: heaviest (6 tons), thickest skin (1 inch), biggest brain (12 pounds), and, of course, longest nose (8 feet). Elephants also make the world's silliest noises in their sleep!

## 7

MAMMALS

### Three-Toed Sloth
**WHERE FOUND:** CENTRAL AND SOUTH AMERICA
**LENGTH:** 2 FEET
**WEIGHT:** 7½ TO 9½ POUNDS

## 8

MAMMALS

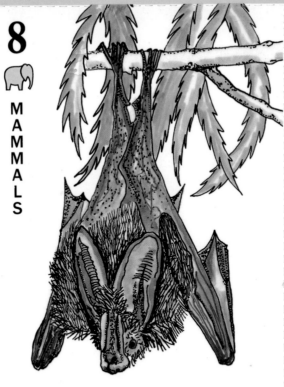

### Bat
**WHERE FOUND:** WORLDWIDE
**WINGSPAN:** 6 INCHES TO 5 FEET
**WEIGHT:** LESS THAN ⅒ OF AN OUNCE TO 2 POUNDS

## 9

MAMMALS

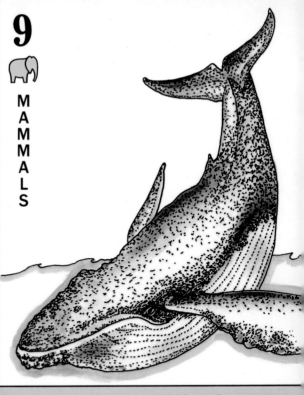

### Humpback Whale
**WHERE FOUND:** ALL OCEANS
**LENGTH:** 40 TO 50 FEET
**WEIGHT:** 25 TO 50 TONS

## 10

MAMMALS

### Cheetah
**WHERE FOUND:** AFRICA, ASIA
**LENGTH:** 4½ FEET
**WEIGHT:** 110 TO 130 POUNDS

## 11

MAMMALS

### Star-Nosed Mole
**WHERE FOUND:** EASTERN NORTH AMERICA
**LENGTH:** 8 INCHES
**WEIGHT:** 2 TO 4 OUNCES

## 12

MAMMALS

### Capybara
**WHERE FOUND:** SOUTH AMERICA
**LENGTH:** 3 TO 4½ FEET
**WEIGHT:** 110 TO 175 POUNDS

# Here's the Record:

### World's Greatest Singer

Humpbacks sing eerie songs that are far too complex for any other animal's voice — including ours!

## Did You Know?

Each year thousands of humpback whales return from the wide oceans to their sheltered winter waters singing a new song. It may be 30 minutes long and full of such sighings, throbbings, thrummings, clickings, and gliding scales that just remembering it all seems impossible. But whales do remember. All the humpbacks in one part of the ocean can repeat that same song, almost as if they are telling a story. And every year the tune is a little different. Why? No one knows.

## Think of This!

Humpbacks have been recorded. You may be able to listen to them at your local library.

# Here's the Record:

### Keenest Hearing

Bats have the world's most advanced kind of "sonar." They can "see" things as small as fruit flies with their ears!

## Did You Know?

Bats aren't blind — as you might have heard — but they find their way around with their ears rather than their eyes. The bat emits a high-pitched sound through its mouth or nostrils. Some of this sound returns as it bounces off objects. With its two super ears, the bat forms a "picture" from these sounds — the same way your eyes use light to tell you the location, shape, or speed of things around you.

## Think of This!

Bracken Cave, near San Antonio, Texas, has the largest concentration of wild mammals anywhere in the world today: 20 million bats!

# Here's the Record:

### Slowest Mammal

A sloth in a hurry can cover just over four yards in one minute, but it normally travels at only half that speed!

## Did You Know?

The sloth prefers not to move at all. It spends its life hanging upside down from a tree branch. Awake for only about six hours each day, it gathers whatever fruit and leaves are within reach. If its food supply holds out, a sloth can stay in the same tree for a lifetime! It even begins to look like its tree home, since, during the rainy season, green plants called algae grow on its long hairs.

## Think of This!

What would it be like to live in slow motion? If you brushed your teeth at top sloth speed each morning, it would take 40 minutes; putting on your shoes would take another 20!

# Here's the Record:

### Largest Rodent

This giant guinea pig look-alike can weigh as much as a 6-foot-tall person!

## Did You Know?

This is *not* the kind of rodent that even an ambitious tabby cat would like to meet. Only jaguars are big enough to play cat-and-mouse with capybaras. When pursued, a capybara usually takes to the water; it dives and swims quite well. At night it shelters in burrows along river banks, so its best escape route flows right by its front door.

## Think of This!

One enemy worries the capybara more than jaguars — we ferocious humans. Capybara meat is eaten in South America; no one thinks it tastes very good, but it's cheap and plentiful.

# Here's the Record:

### Weirdest Nose

This mole has 22 wriggling "tentacles" around its nose.

## Did You Know?

Like tiny, fleshy fingers, the star-nosed mole's feelers are always moving when it patrols its tunnels for food — that is, all except the top two, which stand out stiff and straight. Perhaps they're to warn of cave-ins or other dangers.

Tunneling, especially in damp or marshy ground, is the mole's way of life. Always eating along the way, a mole tours its underground domain once every three or four hours.

## Think of This!

The mole keeps a neat house — or, in this case, mound. As winter nears, you might find a thousand or more worms inside, all laid out for the season ahead in tidy piles of about ten each.

# Here's the Record:

### Fastest Land Animal

A cheetah can sprint at up to 70 miles per hour over short distances!

## Did You Know?

There's no question of the cheetah's record-setting speed. A hungry cheetah pursuing its prey will pull out all the stops, reaching top speed in only a few seconds — faster than even a race car can! But if it fails to run down its prey quickly, the cheetah gives up the chase, exhausted by its burst of speed.

Animal trainers say cheetahs learn faster than other big cats, and Indian princes once exchanged them as favored pets.

## Think of This!

To win a 100-yard dash with a cheetah, the fastest human would need a 70-yard head start!

## Here's the Record:

### Greatest Baby-Sitter

With an egg cradled atop its webbed feet, an emperor father stands motionless through 60 days of the black Antarctic winter.

## Did You Know?

The emperor penguin actually holds many records. Not only is it the largest penguin (48 inches tall) and the deepest bird diver (to 870 feet), but it also has the warmest coat. Greatest by far, however, is the emperor's baby-sitting record. Although temperatures can drop to 110 degrees below zero and gale winds whine through weeks of constant darkness, the father penguin will neither move nor eat until the chick hatches and its mother has returned from the sea.

## Think of This!

How cold is 110 degrees below? Cold enough to turn your breath instantly to ice!

## Here's the Record:

### Smelliest Bird

The hoatzin's strong, musty odor has earned it the nickname "stinkbird."

## Did You Know?

The hoatzin's unpleasant smell is only one of several hoatzin mysteries. Another is the claws that hoatzin chicks have on the edges of their wings! (They use them to clamber up trees.) The chicks swim well, too. Their bald little bodies make them look like strange, winged lizards. And that's an important clue: all modern birds seem to be descended from small hopping dinosaurs. The hoatzin gives us a rare peek at how nature set about changing a dinosaur into a bird.

## Think of This!

If you'd like to see more of nature's blueprints for building birds out of dinosaurs, find a library book on prehistoric creatures and look closely at a character called *Archaeopteryx*.

## Here's the Record:

### Longest-Living Bird

Andean condors may live up to 70 years!

## Did You Know?

Soaring on immense, broad wings, the Andean condor patrols a large patch of sky, its sharp eyes searching the land below for animal carcasses. Although it is the largest of all the condors, this bird poses no threat to living animals. In fact, it is discouraged by anything that moves. The condor's beak is actually quite weak, useful just for pulling at loose, rotted meat. (You can be quite sure that the condor is *not* a finicky eater!)

## Think of This!

If you see a condor at the zoo, notice that its head is altogether bald, the better to poke into dead animals without making a frightful mess of its plumage!

## Here's the Record:

### Longest Migration

Twice a year, this graceful bird makes a trip from one polar region of the world to the other — 12,500 miles each way!

## Did You Know?

Arctic terns spend their summers within the Arctic Circle. Like many northern birds, they must make a long journey when the seasons change. But the tern's flight is the longest: all the way to the Antarctic! How birds can guide themselves to places halfway around the world is still something of a puzzle. Scientists do think, however, that tiny magnetic particles in birds' brains may help — acting like natural compasses.

## Think of This!

Hundreds of years ago, people were even more mystified than we are today by the yearly vanishing of birds. Some thought birds hibernated in shallow mud, as certain crabs do. A few suggested that birds wintered on the moon!

## Here's the Record:

### Largest Bird

Far too heavy to fly, the ostrich weighs as much as 345 pounds and may grow to be an imposing 9 feet tall!

## Did You Know?

Men have made a sport of trying to ride this giant bird and have even trained it to herd sheep. In its mating season, though, the ostrich is not to be trifled with. Stamping and kicking with its huge talons, whipping its long neck from side to side, and charging at up to 40 miles an hour, an ostrich may attack anything — including a locomotive!

## Think of This!

The ostrich also holds the record for laying the bird world's largest egg. If you scrambled just one of these 6-inch-long 9-pounders, you'd have breakfast for fifteen friends!

## Here's the Record:

### Smallest Bird

Weighing less than 1/10 of an ounce, this bird is lighter than some moths!

## Did You Know?

Bee hummingbirds (or "fairy hummers") are 2¼ inches long and live in thimble-sized nests. Like all hummingbirds, they are fantastic fliers, able to dart sideways, up, or down, or hover in the air while dining on flower nectar. Such hardworking fliers need more energy than other animals — not to mention an especially good night's sleep. In fact, hummers practically hibernate each night: their body temperatures can drop 40 degrees while they're asleep!

## Think of This!

Despite their size, hummers have no fear of people. Put a hummingbird feeder in your yard and see for yourself.

# RECORD-SETTING Birds

## 1

### Andean Condor

**WHERE FOUND:** ANDES MOUNTAINS OF SOUTH AMERICA
**LENGTH:** 4 FEET
**WEIGHT:** 20 TO 27 POUNDS

## 2

### Hoatzin

**WHERE FOUND:** SOUTH AMERICA
**LENGTH:** 2 FEET
**WEIGHT:** 1½ POUNDS

## 3

### Emperor Penguin

**WHERE FOUND:** ANTARCTIC COASTS
**HEIGHT:** 4 FEET
**WEIGHT:** 60 TO 100 POUNDS

## 4

### Bee Hummingbird

**WHERE FOUND:** CUBA
**LENGTH:** 2¼ INCHES
**WEIGHT:** LESS THAN ⅟₁₀ OF AN OUNCE

## 5

### Ostrich

**WHERE FOUND:** AFRICA
**HEIGHT:** UP TO 9 FEET
**WEIGHT:** 265 TO 345 POUNDS

## 6

### Arctic Tern

**WHERE FOUND:** ARCTIC AND ANTARCTIC COASTS
**LENGTH:** 16 INCHES
**WEIGHT:** 3½ OUNCES

## Here's the Record:
### Most Talkative Creature
Grey parrots show off with vocabularies of up to 500 words!

## Did You Know?
Grey parrots win more "talking bird" contests than any other bird in the world! They also have musical abilities that many musicians would envy: when the grey parrot repeats a song, it can remember the exact musical key of a previous performance! Of course, even a champion grey parrot doesn't understand a sound it utters. Although it may call other house pets by name or even answer the telephone, it mimics creaking doors and barking dogs with equal satisfaction.

## Think of This!
Parrots learn to imitate sounds only in captivity. In the wild, with no humans to talk to, they merely shriek and squawk!

## Here's the Record:
### Largest Nest
Bald eagle nests can measure 20 feet deep and 9½ feet across!

## Did You Know?
Among mountain crags and high treetops these powerful hunters build their nests. Not only are bald eagle nests the biggest, they're also among the longest-lasting. One eagle family or another may add improvements to the same nest over 20 or 30 years. A really old, gigantic nest may weigh 2 tons! But eagles don't win first prize for engineering. Sooner or later some eagle adds one branch too many, and the whole nest plummets to the ground — with the same impact as dropping an automobile from 100 feet up.

## Think of This!
The bald eagle was adopted in 1782 as our nation's official symbol. Did you know that Benjamin Franklin preferred the wild turkey for that honor?

## Here's the Record:
### Greatest Wingspan
This magnificent flier's wings may span 11 feet, 10 inches from tip to tip!

## Did You Know?
Gliding is an albatross specialty. A wandering albatross can soar on the sea winds for hours without having to flap a wing. It may even nod off for a few moments. No bird, in fact, lives more of its life in the air.

South of the equator, at latitudes called the Roaring Forties, wandering albatross ride the globe-circling air currents, actually flying around the world once every few months!

## Think of This!
You may find a short trip to the grocery store inconvenient; a mother albatross thinks nothing of flying several hundred miles to bring food back to her chicks!

## Here's the Record:
### Keenest Sense of Smell among Birds
A kiwi's nostrils, which are at the tip of its 6-inch-long, flexible beak, can detect food buried several inches underground!

## Did You Know?
Although they are not terribly large by bird standards, kiwis can't fly. Their feathers look more like long fuzz, and their wings are only 2-inch knobs. Completely at home on the ground, kiwis hide in hollows and caves during the day. At night, thrusting their sharp beaks into the earth to sniff around, they use their excellent sense of smell to find insects and worms.

## Think of This!
The kiwi's name comes from the rather weak, shrill cry of the male of the species: "*kee wee kee wee.*" If the bird had been named after the female's call, it would be the "*kurr kurr*"!

## Here's the Record:
### Toughest Bird
Woodpeckers use their bodies as woodworking tools!

## Did You Know?
Any other bird that tried to live a woodpecker's life would quickly knock itself silly, hammering away at trees. But nature designed woodpeckers for toughness. Their heads are thick-boned and cushioned against shock; their short legs and sharp, curved claws give them extra grip; and their specially stiff, strong tail feathers keep them propped upright as they peck for food with their chisel-sharp beaks.

## Think of This!
If you watch a woodpecker, you'll see that it always feeds in the same way. It starts at the bottom of a tree and spirals around the trunk to the top.

## Here's the Record:
### Fanciest Feathers
This family of 43 species includes the most brightly plumed birds in the world!

## Did You Know?
So impressive are these birds' feathers that for hundreds of years traders sold the plumes to dressmakers and hat makers. We'll never know how many magnificent species completely disappeared before laws passed in 1924 saved these stunning creatures from the hunters!

## Think of This!
These beautiful birds make loud, shrill, squawking sounds just like common crows. That's not as surprising as it sounds — birds of paradise and crows are distant cousins!

## 7

BIRDS

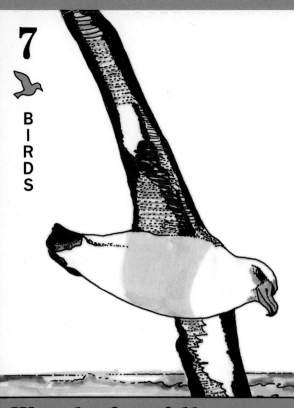

# Wandering Albatross

**WHERE FOUND:** OCEANS OF THE SOUTHERN HEMISPHERE
**WINGSPAN:** UP TO 11 FEET, 10 INCHES
**WEIGHT:** 13 TO 25 POUNDS

## 8

BIRDS

# Bald Eagle

**WHERE FOUND:** UNITED STATES AND CANADA
**LENGTH:** 3½ FEET
**WEIGHT:** 10 TO 14 POUNDS

## 9

BIRDS

# Grey Parrot

**WHERE FOUND:** AFRICA
**LENGTH:** 13 INCHES
**WEIGHT:** LESS THAN 1 POUND

## 10

BIRDS

# Bird of Paradise

**WHERE FOUND:** NEW GUINEA
**LENGTH:** 6 TO 40 INCHES
**WEIGHT:** 3 OUNCES TO 1½ POUNDS

## 11

BIRDS

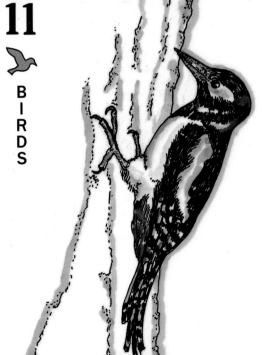

# Woodpecker

**WHERE FOUND:** ALMOST WORLDWIDE
**LENGTH:** 6 TO 18 INCHES
**WEIGHT:** 3 OUNCES TO 1 POUND

## 12

BIRDS

# Kiwi

**WHERE FOUND:** NEW ZEALAND
**HEIGHT:** UP TO 28 INCHES
**WEIGHT:** 2 TO 9 POUNDS

## 1

REPTILES

## 2

REPTILES

## 3

REPTILES

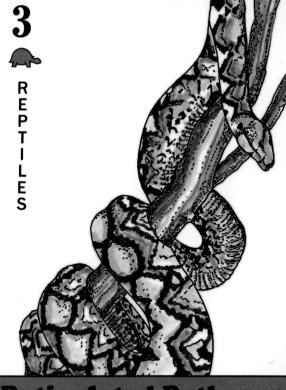

### Salt-Water Crocodile
**WHERE FOUND:** ASIA AND AUSTRALIA
**LENGTH:** UP TO 30 FEET
**WEIGHT:** 900 TO 1,800 POUNDS

### Tuatara
**WHERE FOUND:** ISLANDS OFF NEW ZEALAND
**LENGTH:** 2 FEET
**WEIGHT:** 2 TO 4 POUNDS

### Reticulated Python
**WHERE FOUND:** BURMA, INDONESIA, THE PHILIPPINES
**LENGTH:** UP TO 32 FEET, 9 INCHES
**WEIGHT:** 120 TO 300 POUNDS

## 4

REPTILES

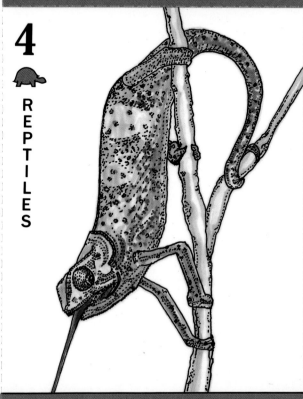

## 5

REPTILES

## 6

AMPHIBIANS

### Chameleon
**WHERE FOUND:** AFRICA, EUROPE, ASIA
**LENGTH:** 4 TO 22 INCHES
**WEIGHT:** LESS THAN 1 OUNCE TO LESS THAN 1 POUND

### Giant Tortoise
**WHERE FOUND:** ISLANDS OF THE INDIAN OCEAN
**LENGTH:** 4½ FEET
**WEIGHT:** 200 TO 300 POUNDS

### Arrow-Poison Frog
**WHERE FOUND:** SOUTH AMERICA
**LENGTH:** ⅓ TO 1 INCH
**WEIGHT:** LESS THAN 1/10 OF AN OUNCE

# Here's the Record:

### Longest Snake

The longest reticulated python ever measured was 32 feet, 9 inches. It weighed just over 300 pounds!

## Did You Know?

Muscular snakes, such as pythons, are called constrictors, since they squeeze their prey to death. For such powerful snakes, eating — not hunting — is the tricky part. A reticulated python's catch may be as large as an antelope; to swallow it, the snake must open its double-hinged jaws as wide as possible and then slowly push its mouth over and around the meal. Having finally engulfed this bulky mouthful, the snake drags itself into the bushes and spends a few days simply digesting its dinner.

## Think of This!

Wondering about the word *reticulated*? It means crisscrossed, like a net — or like the design on the python's back.

# Here's the Record:

### Loneliest Reptile

The sole survivor of a group of ancient beak-headed reptiles, the tuatara escaped extinction and has existed almost unchanged for 200 million years!

## Did You Know?

The tuatara's family used to include many species, some over 6 feet long. They reached their peak about 180 million years ago, whereas dinosaurs reached theirs only 140 million years ago. In that light, the existence today of the unchanged tuatara is perhaps even more astonishing than the existence of live dinosaurs would be. Among the tuatara's prehistoric features is an undeveloped third eye in the middle of its head.

## Think of This!

You have a tiny "third eye," too, but you won't see it in your mirror! It's called the pineal gland, and it's located in the brain.

# Here's the Record:

### Largest Reptile

Salt-water (estuarine) crocs can reach 30 feet in length!

## Did You Know?

These giants of the crocodile family live in the briny waters of coastal inlets, or estuaries. Only the warmest water will do, however; for all their ferocity, crocodiles pass out in cool water.

Because they're so big, salt-water crocs have no problem eating large hunks of food — like you or me, for example. In fact, crocs are awfully good at eating anything they catch: their amazing jaws can close with 13 tons (26,000 pounds) of crushing pressure! Compare this to *your* strongest bite, which has less than 500 pounds of force.

## Think of This!

Zigzag if you're running from a croc. They're fast, but their stumpy legs can't make sharp turns!

# Here's the Record:

### Most Poisonous Creature on Earth

Just 1 ounce of this frog's poison could cause the deaths of more than a million people!

## Did You Know?

There are several kinds of arrow-poison frogs. All are brightly colored, tiny (less than an inch long), and terribly poisonous. A frog called the Kokoi secretes the deadliest of the poisons.

Arrow-poison frogs don't bite; the poison on their skin serves to protect them from their large, hungry enemies. And just so there won't be any mistake, their flashy colors signal danger to would-be frog eaters.

## Think of This!

Many South American Indians have learned to tip their hunting arrows with frog poison. They reckon the skin of one small frog is good for about 50 deadly arrows.

# Here's the Record:

### Longest-Living Vertebrate

Recorded ages of over 100 are not uncommon, and one tortoise lived for *at least* 152 years!

## Did You Know?

The world-record holder, named Marion's tortoise (after the French explorer Marion de Fresne, who found it), was kept as a pet at an army fort on the island of Mauritius. It was fully grown when de Fresne found it in 1766, so it may already have been about 20 years old. This tortoise went blind in 1908 and ten years later accidentally fell to its death through a gun emplacement. After 152 years, the world's birthday champion didn't even die of old age!

## Think of This!

When would you have been born if you were as old as this creature? Let's allow for that extra 20 years and say 1816. There were only 18 states in the USA, and Abe Lincoln was a 7-year-old!

# Here's the Record:

### Best Quick-Change Artist

Each of the more than 80 species of chameleons has the ability to change its color. If you could put them all together to watch their artistry, you'd see sky-blues, yellows, browns, blacks, greens, oranges, and whites!

## Did You Know?

Although chameleons are commonly thought of as camouflage artists, their coloring has more to do with light, temperature, and emotion than with the color of their surroundings. Fortunately, the shades of green and brown they often display help them blend right in. But an angry chameleon may turn black, for instance — certainly a poor color choice for trying to hide among leaves!

## Think of This!

Other chameleon oddities include a sticky tongue that's longer than the creature's whole body, and turretlike eyes that swivel independently of each other!

## 1
FISH

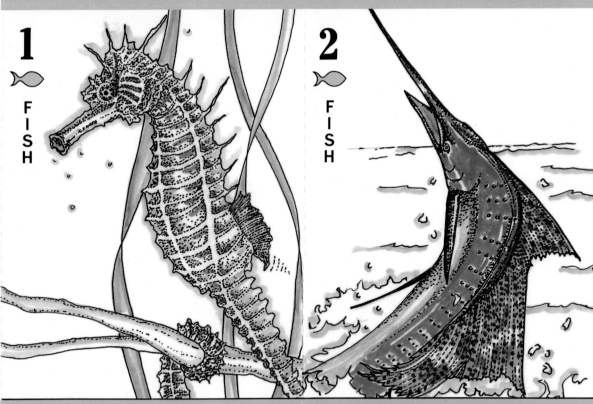

### Seahorse
**WHERE FOUND:** WORLDWIDE
**LENGTH:** 2 TO 12 INCHES
**WEIGHT:** LESS THAN 1 OUNCE

## 2
FISH

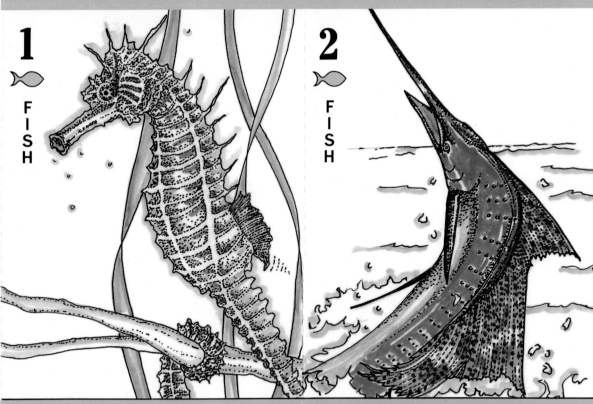

### Sailfish
**WHERE FOUND:** TROPICAL WATERS
**LENGTH:** UP TO 11 FEET
**WEIGHT:** UP TO 221 POUNDS

## 3
FISH

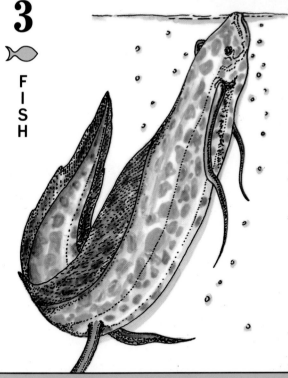

### African Lungfish
**WHERE FOUND:** AFRICA
**LENGTH:** UP TO 6 FEET
**WEIGHT:** UP TO 100 POUNDS

## 4
FISH

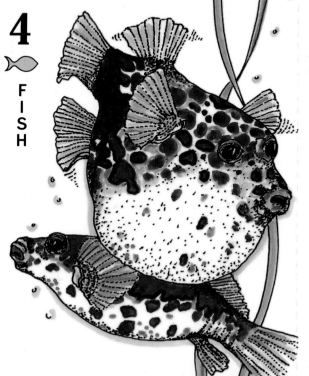

### Death Puffer Fish
**WHERE FOUND:** WESTERN PACIFIC
**LENGTH:** 8 TO 36 INCHES
**WEIGHT:** 14 OUNCES TO 5½ POUNDS

## 5
FISH

### Electric Eel
**WHERE FOUND:** SOUTH AMERICA
**LENGTH:** 5 TO 9 FEET
**WEIGHT:** 30 TO 90 POUNDS

## 6
FISH

### Gulper Eel
**WHERE FOUND:** OCEAN DEPTHS
**LENGTH:** 3 TO 6 FEET
**WEIGHT:** UNKNOWN

## Here's the Record:

### Greatest Sleeper

The lungfish *estivates* (sleeps through the hottest, not the coldest, weather) for up to five years at a time!

## Did You Know?

As you might have guessed from its name, the lungfish has lungs, just like a land animal. As the flooded pools they live in dry up, lungfish wriggle deep into the mud. Here, they fold their bodies in half and prepare slimy, moist cocoons. At the top of the cocoon, they leave a tiny hole to let in just a little air. Although years may pass, the lungfish will sleep in the earth until, one day, flood waters soften their cocoons and wake them into life.

## Think of This!

While a lungfish is estivating, its whole system runs at $\frac{1}{10}$ its normal rate. *Your* deepest sleep doesn't slow your system down to even half its normal rate.

## Here's the Record:

### Fastest Fish

The sailfish can put on bursts of speed up to 68 miles per hour!

## Did You Know?

A sailfish in a hurry tucks its sail fin away, folding it like an accordion in a groove along its back. Why, you may ask, does a 10-foot-long, 200-pound fish have a sail at all? No one is quite sure, but the enormous fin does catch the wind and seems to pull the fish, just like a sailboat, when it lazes on the surface. The fin may also prevent the fish's sleek, torpedo-shaped body from spinning out of control as it tries to slow down after a high-speed dash.

## Think of This!

How do we humans do in the water? Our top speed is about 4½ miles per hour — barely faster than a sea slug!

## Here's the Record:

### Most Unusual Father

A seahorse father protects his mate's eggs in his special pouch for 4 to 5 weeks and then "gives birth" to them.

## Did You Know?

Seahorses are true fish, but they are without question the slowest-moving ones. Unable to go after food in the shallow coastal waters they inhabit, seahorses prefer to hold on to seaweed with their tails while sucking in any food that drifts within their range. In addition to their grasping monkey tails and kangaroo-like pouches, these fish have a famous profile — it looks like a horse.

## Think of This!

Look for seahorses at an aquarium or pet store. If you stare at them for a while, their delicate, fluttering fins seem to spin like propellers.

## Here's the Record:

### Most Stretchable Stomach

A gulper can stuff its stomach until it's more than twice the size of the fish itself!

## Did You Know?

In black, icy waters, 6,000 to 15,000 feet below the ocean's surface, live nightmarish fish. Because there's not much food down there, everybody is anxious to eat everybody else. One of the inhabitants of these depths, the 6-foot-long gulper eel, looks like a pair of menacing jaws with a ribbon of body stuck on just to help the jaws get around. But the gulper's stomach can stretch larger than its whole body! When full, the stomach hangs like a huge balloon underneath the fish. Empty, it shrinks to practically nothing.

## Think of This!

Under the crushing weight of water at 15,000 feet, you'd have to suit up in 2 inches of steel plate to avoid becoming a human pancake!

## Here's the Record:

### Most Shocking Fish

A 90-pound electric eel can generate a giant jolt — 650 volts and 1 amp!

## Did You Know?

Although the world contains a few other kinds of living "batteries," the electric eel generates by far the strongest current. Its special power supply comes from row upon row of small, natural battery cells. They're hooked together for extra power, like batteries in a flashlight.

## Think of This!

How many things around your house could an eel power all at once? Although they would run down very quickly, one eel could turn on a TV, a stereo, two 75-watt lamps, and a vacuum cleaner!

## Here's the Record:

### Most Poisonous Fish

Puffer fish don't bite, but their bodies contain the most dangerous poison of any fish.

## Did You Know?

Puffer poison numbs and slows the body until there is no life left — but that's only if you eat a puffer fish. Actually, puffers give plenty of warning to stay away. When disturbed, they blow themselves up like balloons, tripling their size.

Who, you may ask, would want to eat a deadly inflated balloon? People, that's who! Puffer meat, called *fugu*, is a costly treat in some Japanese restaurants.

## Think of This!

Though *fugu* chefs must spend three years learning how to remove all of the puffer fish's poisonous parts, mistakes still happen. Each year a few people die from eating such mistakes.

# Here's the Record:

### Greatest Insect Gardener

These busy ants grow their own food!

## Did You Know?

Leaf-cutters prefer one tasty fungus to all other foods, so they actually cultivate their own crop in underground chambers. They cut up vast quantities of leaves to use as fertilizer, and they weed out unwanted growths. Of course, since they have razor-sharp jaws, leaf-cutters find this kind of gardening easy work.

## Think of This!

You'll *never* guess what other remarkable use the leaf-cutter's jaws have. People in the tropics apply the insects to wounds, just as a doctor might take stitches. The ants bite the wound's edges together; then the ants' bodies are twisted away, leaving behind a neat row of clamps!

# Here's the Record:

### Heaviest Insect

The hard-plated goliath weighs up to 3½ ounces and measures up to 4¾ inches!

## Did You Know?

What has horns, flies through the air, and weighs as much as a double-scoop ice cream cone? This is no joke, it's the goliath beetle! Like all beetles, it has a hard outer shell made of chitin — a glossy, dark plating — but the goliath's chitin armor grows thicker than that of other beetles.

## Think of This!

How does it feel to be an armored beetle? Well, how do you feel wearing football pads and a plastic helmet? Think of the goliath as being suited up in nature's own plastic, which happens to fit much better than your store-bought safety gear!

# Here's the Record:

### Most Dangerous Creature

Flies spread 30 different serious diseases to people all over the world.

## Did You Know?

Perhaps you imagined the world's most dangerous creature differently — something scaly and huge, with long fangs and glinting scales. The truth is that disease brings more death and misery to humans than any flashy monster ever could. Because flies thrive on a diet of human and other animal waste, their bodies become carriers of harmful bacteria. This is particularly true in the world's poorer countries, where modern sanitation facilities do not exist.

## Think of This!

If just one fly's eggs and all their offspring were allowed to hatch and grow without interference for 6 months, the result would be 5 *trillion* flies — weighing 80,000 tons!

# Here's the Record:

### Longest Insect

These unusual creatures can grow as long as 13 inches!

## Did You Know?

In scientific language, the walkingstick family is known as *phasmida,* which is ancient Greek for "phantom." No wonder! Who can be sure he's seen an insect that looks like a bare twig come to life? But no shape could better protect these night hunters, which must pass the daylight hours concealed in trees. Some walkingsticks can even change color to match their surroundings!

## Think of This!

If you're lucky enough to find a walkingstick and careful enough to keep it as a pet, here's a very strange thing you may wish to know: lightly stroking a walkingstick on its underside will make it go rigid.

# Here's the Record:

### Greatest Spinner

For over 3,500 years, silkworm cocoons have been used to make our finest fabrics!

## Did You Know?

A silkworm caterpillar is really a single-minded machine. Nothing else matters but that it eat, eat, eat to store energy for its amazing transformation into a winged moth. A lot of its diet becomes protein, which is used in spinning the fine thread for its cocoon — an unbroken silk strand up to 3,000 feet long (that's over half a mile!). But the full-grown silkworm moth that emerges from this elegant sleeping bag will only live for three days. It has no mouth!

## Think of This!

Here's an easy way to tell moths from butterflies: with few exceptions, butterflies flutter during the day; moths are active only at night!

# Here's the Record:

### Greatest Jumper

A flea can jump almost 130 times its own height!

## Did You Know?

Getting 7 or 8 inches off the ground may not seem like much to you, but it's pretty amazing for a creature less than 1/16 of an inch tall. Fleas' special hind legs snap straight with the aid of a natural rubber band that's stretched between their upper joints. If fleas weren't built like catapults, they would starve. They feed on our mammal blood, and they have to make quick, high jumps to get to their next meal!

## Think of This!

The human Olympic high-jump record is only 1.2 times the jumper's height. To compete with a flea, you would have to jump more than 800 feet — as high as a 60-story skyscraper.

## 1

INSECTS

### Fly
**WHERE FOUND:** WORLDWIDE
**LENGTH:** ⅛ TO ¼ INCH
**WEIGHT:** LESS THAN ¹⁄₁₀₀ OF AN OUNCE

## 2

INSECTS

### Goliath Beetle
**WHERE FOUND:** EQUATORIAL AFRICA
**LENGTH:** UP TO 4¾ INCHES
**WEIGHT:** UP TO 3½ OUNCES

## 3

INSECTS

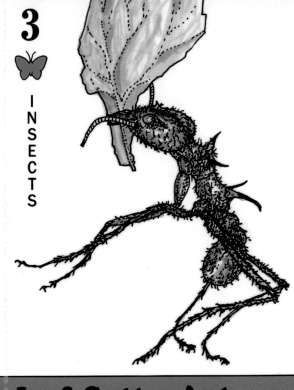

### Leaf-Cutter Ant
**WHERE FOUND:** SOUTHERN U.S. TO S. AMERICA
**LENGTH:** ¹⁄₁₆ TO 1 INCH
**WEIGHT:** LESS THAN ¹⁄₁₀₀ OF AN OUNCE

## 4

INSECTS

### Flea
**WHERE FOUND:** WORLDWIDE
**HEIGHT:** ¹⁄₁₆ INCH
**WEIGHT:** LESS THAN ¹⁄₁₀₀ OF AN OUNCE

## 5

INSECTS

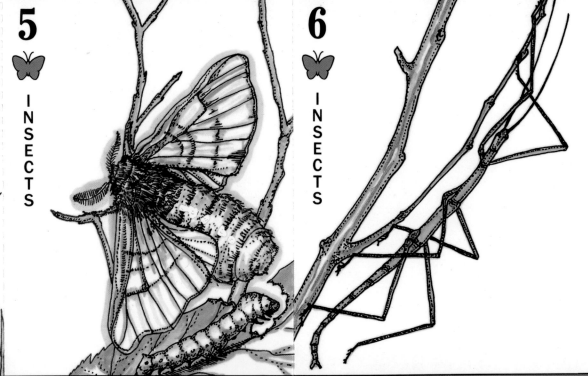

### Silkworm Moth
**WHERE FOUND:** ASIA
**WINGSPAN:** 2 INCHES
**WEIGHT:** LESS THAN ¹⁄₁₀ OF AN OUNCE

## 6

INSECTS

### Walkingstick
**WHERE FOUND:** WORLDWIDE
**LENGTH:** 2 TO 13 INCHES
**WEIGHT:** LESS THAN ¹⁄₁₀ OF AN OUNCE

# Here's the Record:

*Most Legs of Any Creatures*

Although no millipede ever quite lives up to its name ("thousand feet"), it may get around on as many as 700 legs!

## Did You Know?

A millipede is put together a bit like a train. Take one simple part — a short body segment with its own four legs — hook together as many as 175 of these pieces, and you've created a millipede.

## Think of This!

Don't pick up a millipede to count its legs. These creatures aren't poisonous, as centipedes are, but the ooze from their stink glands can give you an unpleasant burn. Besides, are you *sure* it's a millipede and not a centipede?

# Here's the Record:

*Oddest Insect Defense*

When they're disturbed, these beetles fire themselves like tiny cannons!

## Did You Know?

Many insects protect themselves with armor, speed, or disguise, but only bombardiers have their own artillery! These beetles mix ingredients inside a special body tube, then shoot a foul-smelling mist rearward with a sudden, noisy "pop." A bombardier can fire as many as 29 shots in 4 minutes, and its aim — pointing backward — is excellent!

## Think of This!

Beware! A bombardier's cloud not only smells awful, it's also boiling hot! You might get hurt if you get too close.

# Here's the Record:

*Largest Butterfly*

This rare birdwing butterfly lifts itself into the air on broad wings that may span up to 11 inches.

## Did You Know?

Queen Alexandra birdwings don't like to come down from their jungle treetops. Since they have such large, delicate wings, there is great danger of injury for them in brush and branches. So forget about going after this specimen with a net — unless you can fly, too!

## Think of This!

Butterfly wings are made of scales that are so light and flexible that butterflies skitter on the breeze like natural kites.

# Here's the Record:

*Biggest Spider*

Bird-eaters measure 10 inches, including their outstretched legs; their bodies are 3½ inches long!

## Did You Know?

Husky, hairy spiders like the bird-eater are less dangerous than they look. You would find the bird-eater's bite no more unpleasant than a bee sting, though its body hairs would irritate your skin if you handled one! The bird-eater's favorite dwelling is any tunnel left by a burrowing rodent; this giant spider lines the tunnel with silk to make it into a more comfortable home. At night it hunts, overpowering even tiny animals and small birds!

## Think of This!

People occasionally make pets of large spiders (they can live 15 years or longer), but no one has ever reported being able to teach them any tricks.

# Here's the Record:

*Largest Spider Web*

The tropical orb weaver's yellow silk webs may stretch 15 feet across!

## Did You Know?

The neat, taut spirals of the tropical orb weaver's webs are often densely strung from tree to tree in forest and jungle. This strong, elastic spider silk can be pulled to twice its length before it breaks. Small animals have little chance in such a sticky, stretchy trap, and even humans find it hard going to crash through one tough, springy web after another. Natives use the threads to fashion both fishing nets and hats!

## Think of This!

The next time you're admiring a perfect web, and the spider doesn't seem to be at home, look around for a thin "signal" strand. You may find the web's owner concealed nearby, at the other end of its alarm device.

# Here's the Record:

*Most Venomous Scorpion*

This desert-dweller's sting can kill a person in 4 hours!

## Did You Know?

The great Sahara desert is home to many poisonous snakes, but its human inhabitants worry more about 7-inch-long scorpions. These monsters possess a venom that is similar to a cobra's, and they like to creep into clothing and shoes at night. Scorpions sting to catch food, but also out of fright — so if a scorpion has bedded down in your belongings, getting dressed in the morning can be a rude awakening for both of you! When they're not lurking in your wardrobe, scorpions hunt insects and don't object to an occasional lizard or mouse.

## Think of This!

A scorpion strikes by arching its tail stinger over its back and stabbing forward. Treat even the smallest scorpion with respect: they are fast, and all have nasty stings.

## 7
INSECTS

### Queen Alexandra
**WHERE FOUND:** PAPUA NEW GUINEA
**WINGSPAN:** UP TO 11 INCHES
**WEIGHT:** UP TO ½ OUNCE

## 8
INSECTS

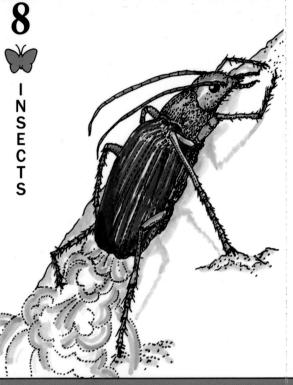

### Bombardier Beetle
**WHERE FOUND:** NORTH AMERICA, AFRICA, ASIA
**LENGTH:** ¼ INCH TO 1½ INCHES
**WEIGHT:** LESS THAN 1/10 OF AN OUNCE

## 9
INSECT RELATIVES

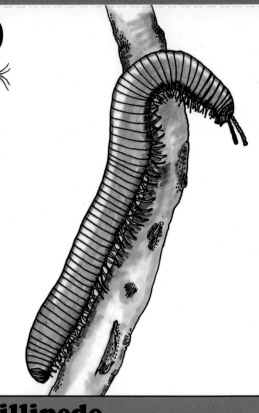

### Millipede
**WHERE FOUND:** WORLDWIDE
**LENGTH:** 1/10 INCH TO 11 INCHES
**WEIGHT:** UP TO 2 OUNCES

## 10
INSECT RELATIVES

### N. African Scorpion
**WHERE FOUND:** NORTH AFRICA
**LENGTH:** UP TO 7 INCHES
**WEIGHT:** UP TO 1 OUNCE

## 11
INSECT RELATIVES

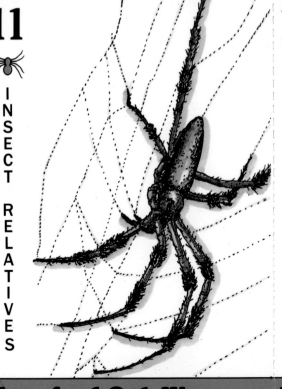

### Tropical Orb Weaver
**WHERE FOUND:** TROPICS
**LENGTH:** ½ INCH TO 2 INCHES
**WEIGHT:** LESS THAN 1/10 OF AN OUNCE

## 12
INSECT RELATIVES

### Bird-Eating Spider
**WHERE FOUND:** SOUTH AMERICA
**LENGTH:** UP TO 10 INCHES
**WEIGHT:** UP TO 2½ OUNCES